THE BOOK OF BRIAN

BRIAN BERT

Explanation of the cover:
The ring with the Magen David belonged to my great grandfather. He gave this to my father on the occasion of his Barmitzvah. Just before my father died, he gave me the ring for safekeeping.

The second ring is my wedding ring. Lindsay and I have now been together for close to half a century. Feels like a day!

"The Book of Brian," by Brian Bert. ISBN 978-1-63868-049-9 (softcover).

Published 2022 by Virtualbookworm.com Publishing Inc., P.O. Box 9949, College Station, TX 77842, US. ©2022, Brian Bert. All rights reserved. No part of this publication may be reproduced, stored in a retrieval system, or transmitted in any form or by any means, electronic, mechanical, recording or otherwise, without the prior written permission of Brian Bert.

Dedicated to Lindsay

My wife, friend, co-traveler and gift.

Introduction

I had the pleasure of knowing some of you, but most of you will be born long after I am gone and a faded memory. So I have decided to leave this fingerprint for you, a personal gift, and hope that you will find it to be a curiosity and entertaining at the least.

I never knew my grandfathers. They died long before I was born. I did however have the great fortune to be born into a home where both my grandmothers were already living. These two, Debi and Razil lived in the most tumultuous of times during the 20th century. Both experienced wars, emigration, premature deaths of family members and many more trials and tribulations. The latter part of their lives were wonderful though living under the tutelage of my father and mother who loved and protected them both until their deaths at ripe old ages.

I benefitted greatly from their presence, both so full of experience, wisdom, advice and guidance. To this day, I hear their voices in my mind and often conduct the way I navigate the waters around me accordingly. The problem is, that they left no paper trail, or to be more modern, electronic fingerprints and so all that they were, all their thoughts, experiences and wisdom were lost with them.

I have often thought how wonderful it would be if any of my grandparents, not to mention my great grandparents, had jotted down some of their thoughts on paper for me to read, irrespective of how trivial or mind-blowing they may have been. I could have gleamed a glimpse as to who they were and how they thought even though they died long before I was born in most cases. I really feel the void of not having known them.

A short biography

I was born in Johannesburg in the second half of the 20th century in 1954. It was a time when we had no television and certainly no computers. Man landed on the moon for the first time when I was a young teenager. My grandparents came from Lithuania and England. My parents were born in South Africa. I have three siblings, Leonard, Philip and Adele. I met Lindsay my wife, born in Cape town, when she was just 17. We married in 1977 and have been happily together ever since. We have three children, Daniel, Jonathan and Debi. To date we now have seven grandchildren. Like my father, I studied to be a Pharmacist. Like both my parents I felt a close affinity to Israel and the Jewish people ever since I can remember.

After the Roman destruction of Jerusalem 2000 years ago, the Jewish people were dispersed to all corners of the globe. They had to put up with severe discrimination and persecution wherever they went. For 2000 years, they would pray in their synagogues "next year in Jerusalem". Six years before I was born, the modern State of Israel came into being. The magnetic pull was very powerful and already, at the tender age of ten, I informed my parents that I intended to go live in Israel to help build the fledgling Jewish state. In 1984, after our second child Jonathan was born, we left beautiful Africa for a relatively primitive, under-developed Israel. It warms my heart today to see what a miraculous country it has developed into and I am very glad that my grandchildren speak Hebrew and now have the privilege of living in their own country, safe and free of persecution.

Some of my observations about life:

- The background tapestry to life is pressure. This is a preprogrammed condition for all species, without which they could not continue to survive. This is a basic tenant to nature and an integral element of existence. You were born, or more to the point, woven into this tapestry.

- Life is also completely random. It's like a hosepipe flaying around in all directions, some are unlucky and get wet, others are fortunate enough to be missed out. It can be very fickle and turn around on a dime! He who goes through life not expecting hardships, problems and heartbreaks from time to time, is in complete denial of reality. Of- course one can also look forwards to wonderful times with great excitement, pride and achievement.

- Balance is the most important word in life. Everything needs to be in balance, especially relationships. Excess in any form, is toxic and can be very destructive.

- They say that one of the main factors in the success of a retail business is position, position, position. Similarly, we can say that for success in life it's: attitude, attitude and attitude.

- Radiate happiness, kindness and optimism and that's exactly how others will relate back to you. Life is a mirror after all. Smile at it and it will smile back at you!

- Music and humor are two of the main lubricants to life. They really ease the way and make the journey so much more pleasant.

- The ability to put life in perspective is a very helpful trait. This stimulates the desire not to waste time or opportunity and therefore facilitate the harboring of no regrets in the end. Life is really short!

- You have the gift of all your senses. Use them well. Embrace them, don't take them for granted! Consciously stop yourself from time to time and remind yourself to appreciate in real time all that you are sensing.

- Don't vacillate, especially in health matters, act as soon as possible and with confidence. "He who waits is lost."

- Be inquisitive of all things. Hold an open mind. Constantly asking and learning. Pursue your own, unique, individual thoughts. So many people live their whole lives without producing one single unique thought of their own.

- Try as much as possible to eradicate the words "I" and "me" from your lexicon, be humble - people react poorly to selfishness and ego.

- Speaking clearly and eloquently is important. A high EQ (emotional quotient) is always helpful. Can be as important as IQ. The more languages one can speak the better. These open so many doors and opportunities!

Now the big questions. Where are we? Why are we alive?

I have pondered these questions literally my whole life. Clearly, no one can ever know with certainty, but I put before you two ideas to ponder: I am sure you have many of your own ideas too!

1) The universe may be part of a living body. Specifically, part of a nervous or blood system. Life, may have one or more functions in this body: genetic material (such as messenger RNA), chemical transmitters as found in neurons or energy converters, similar to ATP molecules. All of these scenarios, would neatly explain the cycle of life, ending in a death.

2) Alternatively, Schlichut is a Hebrew word meaning to be sent on a mission. Our real permanent existence may occur in a realm we inhabit before life and after death. Let's, for the sake of illustration, call this realm heaven. Heaven has some realities to it and one of them is the need for sustenance, energy, fuel and nutrition. The energies needed are derived from many sources and one of these may be supplemented by our living. We absorb all kinds of energies and by living we may convert them into "spiritual energy" which is harvested and transmitted to heaven.

In this capacity, I have no idea how many times we would be called upon to go on schlichut or what the frequency would be, but life could well be one of the many critical sources needed to keep heaven energized.

If any of these scenarios I have laid out above were to be accurate then it would mark our existence as being of significance.

Would love to have had the opportunity to read your ideas on this subject?

The future as I see it

Medicine has made great leaps and bounds and just recently we have begun to understand how to use our own bodies to self- heal. Genetic manipulation, cloning, 3D printing of body parts are a few of the newly discovered modalities. I predict the end to all invasive medicine such as having procedures like operations and opening the body. I believe that all treatments will be virtual and non- invasive and that our present average lifespan of 85 years will rise most probably to 120 years.

When I was a young boy, the limits to our knowledge concerning the universe was that there were two known galaxies, our Milky way and Adromeda - our sister galaxy. We also could identify a few thousand stars and placed them in patterns called the constellations. Our main challenge was to get to the other planets in our solar system, but the technology wasn't yet available.

Now towards the end of my life we now know that there are more galaxies in our universe than all the grains of sand on all the beaches in the world! We can pin the age of our universe to just over 13 billion years with accuracy. We can actually identify the remnants of the first "Big Bang". The birth of our universe. We are presently hearing theories that there are more universes out there. -Parallel universes.

The two big challenges that still lie ahead of us at this stage, are discovering a way to travel at much higher speeds, allowing us to discover new planets that may allow us to colonize and live on them. The importance here is that we are destroying our own environment at such a pace that in the distant future, the earth may not be a viable place to live on anymore. The second challenge is to find proof of life somewhere out there. To date we have not had any sign of this. I suspect that in your lifetimes it will be a proven fact, that there are more life forms in the universe than all the galaxies!

As I write, humanity still has an intrinsic problem in that its intelligence and knowledge are outstripping its pace of evolution. The implication is an inability to absorb, channel, and control resultant technologies. We are on the cusp now of AI (artificial intelligence) technology taking root. Who knows if we will be able to control this once it's let loose! This is analogous to a baby being given a loaded gun to play with.

Unfortunately, our evolution has been held back by factors such as religion, which I believe, in time will be proven to be the most negative, deleterious and destructive force in man's history.

The interplay and consistency across the whole universe of chemistry, physics, biology and mathematics to create all that we know has always been and remains an absolute marvel to me.

Blessing
To all my kin who follow me: I wish you lives that are exciting, rewarding, filled with love and enlightenment. That you will, at a young age, so as not to waste your youth, realize what a wonderful and unique gift your life is. That as you reach the end of your journey, you will harbor no guilt or regrets and find absolute peace of mind.

Brian Bert 1954 – (hopefully, somewhere around 2054)

What follows is a random selection of my thoughts as they appeared to me over my lifetime.

I started recording these already at the young age of 16 and continue to this day.

The selection is in no particular order as to importance or chronology.

My father was a very active spiritual medium and apparently, I have the propensity to be the same. Unlike him however, I have no interest in pursuing this course of action, since I believe that we have to live our physical lives to the full and without such distractions.

This being said, you will notice there is a strong element of spirituality to many of my thoughts and writings.

Hope you enjoy!

HELPING HAND
THE ACT OF CHARITY TO A FRIEND
IS A RELATIONSHIP SMITTEN,
FOR IT IS WELL KNOWN
THAT THE HAND WHICH FEEDS
IS ALWAYS THE HAND THAT IS BITTEN.

LOST

THE ROAD OF LIFE
WITH ITS UPS AND DOWNS
TWISTS AND TURNS
HAS BEEN WELL WORN
TRODDEN BY MANY
IT GOES IN ONE DIRECTION AND
HAS NEITHER DETOUR, DEVIATION, NOR
INTERSECTION,
NO GOING BACKWARDS OR OVER THE EDGE
NO MARKING TIME EITHER
TO CATCH ONE'S BREATH,
JUST RELENTLESSLY FORWARDS,
AT ALL COSTS.
AND YET, INCOHERENTLY, ON THIS ROAD
WE ALL FEEL SO CONFUSED
AND SO UTTERLEY LOST.

DODO
THE SPIRIT MOVED OVER THE WATERS,
THE LAND AND ALL OF THE FERMANENT,
IT SEARCHED BOTH HIGH AND LOW
AND NOW IT WANTS TO KNOW
WHAT HAVE WE DONE WITH ITS DODO?

PHILOSOPHY
SO THE QUESTION IS
DO YOU KEEP YOUR EYES
FIXED AND FOCUSSED ON THE TARGET
OR DO YOU LET THEM STRAY
AND ENJOY THE BEAUTY
ALONG THE WAY?

ASH TO ASH
A MILLION MOURNERS
BUT NOT ONE TEAR,
FOR THE STENCH OF POWER
AND MONEY WAS HERE.

AFFLUENCE
COMFORT AND PRIVELDGE
DULL THE SENSES WITH HASTE
AND IN TIME, EVEN THE CAVIAR
LOSES ITS TASTE.

MY BROTHER

WHAT CAN I SAY TO YOU
DYING SO YOUNG, MY BROTHER, MY DEAR FRIEND?
BE STRONG, BE BRAVE,
THAT WE ALL GO THE SAME WAY IN THE END?
NO, THESE ARE THE WORDS OF COWARDS,
I'D RATHER TELL YOU THE TRUTH
THAT WHEN I LOOK AT YOU
I AM SCARED, FRUSTRATED AND ANGRY
AT THIS CRUEL INJUSTICE
AND THAT WHEN WE ARE FINALLY RIPPED APART
CHEATED BY DEATH,
THERE WILL REMAIN AN OPEN WOUND
ONE THAT WILL NEVER SCAR,
FOR IT WILL WEEP FOREVER
AND IF IT PLEASES GOD, YOU WILL FIND PEACE
AND SOLACE WHEREVER YOU ARE,
BUT I WON'T, NOT UNTIL WE MEET AGAIN
FOR TRULY, I AM YOUR BROTHER,
I AM YOUR DEAR FRIEND.

LIFE
STRUGGLE AND STRIFE ARE
OUR GLUCOSE, OUR ENGINE WITHIN.
CONTENTMENT IS ITS NEMISIS,
IT'S INSULIN.

INHERITANCE
PARENTS WOUNDS
OFTEN APPEAR
AS CHILDRENS SCARS.

THE STONE
FINALLY I HAVE FOUND
THE ROSETTA STONE TO LIFE,
DECIPHERED, IT READS
S-E-L-F-I-S-H

RESPECT
RESPECT COMES FROM
THINKING TWICE AND
SPEAKING ONCE.

DEATH
I HAVE NO PROBLEM WITH DEATH
I KNOW MANY WHO WENT THERE BEFORE ME
TO DATE, I'VE HEARD OF NO COMPLAINTS
SEEN NO RETURNS
NOR ANY CANCELATIONS.

CANCER

"BE STRONG! NOT TO WORRY! ALL WILL BE OK!"
SO WHICH AM I, THE CLOWN OR THE FOOL?
CAN'T YOU SEE THAT I AM DYING HERE!
WHO WILL REALLY SPEAK WITH ME?
HELP ME TO PROCESS THIS FATE SO CRUEL?

REFLECTIONS
WHEN YOU LOOK IN THE MIRROR
HOPE YOU LIKE THE SIGHT
FOR THAT IS THE ONLY FRIEND
WHO'S GOING TO ACCOMPANY YOU
THROUGH THE DARKNESS,
AND INTO THE LIGHT.

PSYCHOLOGY
FORGET THE I IN ME
AND FOCUS ON THE U IN THEM
AND YOU WILL NEVER WALK
ALONE.

DUST
DUST ON THE VERANDA,
THAT'S WHO WE ARE
WITH NO PERSPECTIVE
OF TIME OR SCALE
NOT EVEN A NOTION
AS TO WHERE WE ARE.

HEAVEN
MANAGED TO PEEP BEHIND THE CURTAIN
TO LOOK DEEP INTO THE LIGHT
THEY SAY "REST IN PEACE"
BUT NOT BEHIND THIS WINDOW
CERTAINLY NOT ON THIS NIGHT!

ISIAH - Déjà vu
THE SPIRIT MOVED OVER JERUSALEM
THROUGH THE ANCIENT ALLEYS
WADIS AND HILLS
NOW FEELING TIRED AND FROZEN
IT WANTS TO KNOW
WHO ARE THESE PEOPLE?
WHERE ARE MY CHOSEN?

RANDOM
RANDOM LIFE
DELIVERS BOTH GOOD AND BAD
IN EQUAL MEASURE
SO AS THE PENDULUM SWINGS
IT'S PURE CHANCE
THAT DETERMINES MOST THINGS.

THE MISCONCEPTION
THE ONLY WAY
TO SUSTAIN LIFE
IS BY THE STRONG LEADING
AND THE WEAK BEING GIVEN NO BERTH.
AND THERE I WAS THINKING
THAT THE MEEK WOULD INHERIT
THE EARTH?

THINK FIRST
THE ANGRY WORD ONCE SPOKEN
IS INDELIBLE
OFTEN OPENING CHASMS
THAT ARE UNBRIDGABLE.

PATENTS
YES IT'S TRUE
THERE AREN'T ANSWERS TO ALL QUESTIONS
THERE AREN'T SOLUTIONS TO ALL PROBLEMS,
THERE AREN'T REASONS FOR ALL THINGS
THERE'S NO PROMISING A HAPPY ENDING,
FOR LIFE, IT APPEARS,
IS STILL IN THE LABORATORY
PATENTS ARE STILL PENDING.

HYPOCRITS
THESE THEN ARE MY JUDGES
ROOTLESS THEN AND SPINELESS NOW,
STILL CONDESCENDINGLY EXAMINING
THE SWEAT ON MY BROW.

POWER
ALL POWER TO THE RIVER
ON ITS MAIDEN VOYAGE
BUT WE,
SURFING ITS IRRESITABLE CURRENT
HAVE BEEN HERE BEFORE,
AND WE KNOW
THAT AN EVEN GREATER POWER
AWAITS US AT THE SHORE.

CYCLE
AS MEMORIES ALL FADE,
THE SOUL
FILLED WITH LIFE'S NECTAR
IS NOW READY TO ENGAGE
LIKE A BEE RETURNING
FRESH FROM THE GLADE

ALL THAT SHINES
THE SILVER SCREEN
THE GOLDEN GLOBE
POLISHED STEEL
PLATINUM, COPPER
BRASS AND CHROME

LIQUID CRYSTAL
METALLIC SHEEN
PRISMS, SPECTRUMS
SCINTILANT LIGHT
AND LAZER BEAMS

GLISTENING DEW
SHOWERED WITH SNOW
SHIMMERING LAKES
WITH FIREFLIES AGLOW

MOON SHINE
TWINKLING STARS
SKIES OF BRILLIANT BLUE
GOLDEN SUNSETS
WITH SEAS AZURE

GLAZING ON TOP
SPRINKLED WITH SUGAR ICE
CRYSTALS GLINTING
THE TWINKLING IN YOUR EYES
DOLCE VITA BABY
IT'S SO GOOD TO BE ALIVE!

FAIT ACCOMPLI
LITTLE RAINDROP
SITTING COMFORTABLY
ON YON SHADEY LEAF
GLISTENING BRILLIANTLY
PRISMS DANCING WITHIN
A RESPITE, A BLESSED RELIEF
FROM THE STORM
BUT THE THIRSTY RIVER
RAGING BELOW
IS WAITING PATIENTLY
FOR IT KNOWS
THAT IN THE END
THE WIND ALWAYS BLOWS.

JUST ONE DROP
WHAT DIFFERENCE DOES ONE
DROP OF WATER MAKE TO A RIVER?
HARD TO SEE
FUNDAMEMNTAL DILEMA,
FOR BOTH YOU AND ME.

DETOUR
SOMETIMES WE NEED TO
STEP BACK
TO PROGRESS FORWARDS
GO AROUND
TO ADVANCE FURTHER ON
SEARCH WITHIN
TO FIND THE REASON
AND THEN MAYBE
EVEN FIND THE BEYOND.

GREEN LIGHT
IF YOU CAN LOOK BACK
WITH SATISFACTION
AND FORWARDS
WITH ANTICIPATION
THEN YOU ARE EXACTLY
WHERE YOU SHOULD BE
SAME PULSE, SAME DIRECTION
NO HESITATION.

DISSAPOINTMENT
I WAS BORN INTO THE
"LIGHT UNTO THE NATIONS"
TURNS OUT TO BE A CANDLE
FLICKERING IN A STORM

THE MOMENT
GOD OR EVOLUTION
WHAT'S THE DIFFERENCE?
YOUR LIFE IS SUCH A UNIQUE EVENT
A ONE- TIME ONLY GIFT
NEVER TO BE REPEATED AGAIN
DON'T WASTE A SINGLE MOMENT
ABSORB IT ALL, ENJOY EVERY SECOND
DON'T ALLOW IGNORNACE OF
THE DESTINATION
DIVERT YOUR ATTENTION.

THE WAY IT IS
THEY ALL PASS
THE GOOD DAYS,
THE BAD ONES TOO
THE BEGINNING, THE JOURNEY
AND THE END
THEY ALL PASS
AND FINALLY
IT'S ONLY YOU.

CATALYSTS
SOME SAY THAT WE ARE
MADE IN HIS IMAGE
AND ARE DNA
OTHERS THAT WE ARE CHEMICALS
ON A NEURAL PATHWAY
YET WE COULD BE HORMONES
ENZYMES OR IMMUNO PROTEINS TOO
EACH WITH VERY POWERFUL SWAY
WHATEVER THE CASE,
GOOD TO BE PART OF THIS BODY
WARM IN HERE, I INTEND TO STAY!

SLEEP
JUST AS THE EARTH TURNS
INTO THE CHILL OF WINTER
SO MY SOUL SHIVERS
AS GOD TURNS TO REST.

NECTAR
THE SOUL ENTERS THE WORLD
NAKED AND EMPTY
FILLED BY LIFE
IT LEAVES WITH
GOD'S NECTAR.

ROUTE
GOD IS THE SOURCE
LIFE THE RIVER
DEATH IS THE OCEAN.

FLOW
THE STREAM DETERMINES THE FLOW
WE THE FLOTSAM HAVE NO CHOICE
BUT TO FOLLOW.

PLAYING FIELD
BALANCE IN ALL THINGS
IS THE KEY
PEACE OF MIND
THE GOAL

FATHER
I AM YOUR FATHER
YOUR GUIDE IN LIFE
UNQUALIFIED`
INEXPERIENCED
THERE'S NO MANUAL
DON'T KNOW THE ROUTE
THERE'S NO MAP
HOLD MY HAND.

SPACE
FILL THE SPACE AND TIME
ALLOTED TO YOU
WITH LIGHT
FOR THERE ARE
SHADOWS WAITING
TO FILL THEM FOR YOU.
WAITING OUT OF SIGHT.

WRITTEN

IT'S WRITTEN IN THE STARS
IT'S WRITTEN IN STONE
WRITINGS EVEN ON THE WALL
NO SAYING YOU DIDN'T KNOW.

LAWN
ADMIRE THE LAWN
BUT FORGET NOT THE BLADE
OF GRASS.

AMEN
AMEN TO THE SUN ON MY BACK
AND STARS IN MY EYES.

THIRST
ONLY LOVE
CAN QUENCH
THE THIRSTY SOUL.

TOUGH
IT'S DIFFICULT TO GO
INTO THE COLD FORBODING NIGHT
WITH THE WARMTH OF THE SUN
STILL ON YOUR BACK.

MIRROR
LIFE IS LIKE A MIRROR
SMILE AT IT AND IT
WILL SMILE BACK AT YOU.
(Debe Bert 1893-1974)

LITTLE MAN

LITTLE MAN- SPECK OF DUST
WHAT GIVES YOU THE RIGHT
TO DEMAND AND LUST
COSMIC PARTICAL ON AN ETHEREAL WIND
YOUR'E A FLEETING THOUGHT
A SILLY WHIM.

LITTLE MAN STRUTTING THROUGH LIFE
WHAT GIVES YOU THE RIGHT
TO CREATE SUCH STRIFE
FLASH IN A PAN, AN ABOMINATION
FLOATING ETERNALLY
WITH NO DESTINATION

LITTLE MAN SO PATHETICALLY SMALL
WHAT GIVES YOU THE RIGHT
OF CONTROL OVER ALL
IRRELAVENT VIBRATION, ACCIDENT FOR SURE
NATURES VIOLATION
WITH NO KNOWN CURE.

JERUSALEM
JERUSALEM
NAVEL OF THE EARTH
UMBILICAL CORD
SPIRITUAL VORTEX
MAGNETIC CORE.

HOME
MY LOVE IS IN JERUSALEM
BUT MY HEART ROAMS FREE
IN THE BUSHVELD.

ONE LIFE
YOU CAN ONLY LIVE
ONE LIFE AT A TIME
AND CERTAINLY
NOT SOMEONE ELSE'S

GO

GO TO THE RIVER TO DRINK
IT CANNOT COME TO YOU
CLIMB THE MOUNTAIN
TO SEE THE VIEW
IN CANNOT COME TO YOU
TURN TO THE LIGHT
TO FIND GOD
HE COMETH NOT TO YOU.

COMPANY
WHEN THE STORM BUILDS
ON THE BLACK HORISON
AND THE CHILL WIND
SHIVERS YOUR SKIN
THE NOISE AND WARMTH
OF HUMANITY
CAN BE A DAMN FINE THING.

COMA

LIGHT, COMFORTING LIGHT IS ON ITS WAY
WITH ALL ITS COLOURS AND SUBTLE HUES
DRILLING AND PUNCHING HOLES
IN THE DARK
WHICH IS SURROUNDING YOU.

AT FIRST IT MAY BE DISTURBIBG
INTERMITTENT, FLASHY AND NEW
BUT DON'T TAKE FRIGHT
EVEN AS IT INCREASES IN INTENSITY
BECOMING VERY BRIGHT.
YIELD AND SUCUMB TO ITS LURE
LET IT GUIDE YOU UP, UP, UP
LIKE A BIRD IN FLIGHT
GRACEFUL AND SURE.
UP, UP, UP TO WHERE THE NIGHT FADES
IN THE DAWN'S SPREADING LIGHT
FOR THERE YOU WILL FIND US WAITING
SLOWLY, OH SO SLOWLY,
COMING INTO SIGHT

RETISCENCE

A PASSING SHADOW TOLD ME
SOMETHING WAS WRONG
SO WE MET IN YOUR DREAMS
YOU AND ME,
AT FIRST RELAXED AND ALL AT EASE
THAT IS UNTIL I NOTICED
THAT YOU WERE NOT ALONE
NO, NOT JUST YOU,
BUT ANOTHER THREE.
NOW I UNDERSTAND
WHY YOU SLEEP SO DEEP
HANGING ON TO EACH OTHER
NOT WANTING ONE
OR THE OTHER TO LEAVE
BUT GOOD GENTLEMEN
IT'S TIME FOR LAST GOODBYES
SO THAT YOU CAN TURN TOWARDS THE
LIGHT
AND THERE FIND YOUR
EVERLASTING PEACE.

WORRY
SO MUCH TIME AND ENERGY WASTED
WORRYING ABOUT THINGS
THAT NEVER HAPPEN.

JUSTICE

I SWEAR THERE'S NO JUSTICE
THE LEAVES ARE BATHING
IN THE WARM SUNSHINE
DANCING WITH THE BREEZE
HOSTING THE MOST EXOTIC
BIRDS AND FLOWERS
WITH ABSOLUTE EASE
WHILST THE ROOTS ARE STRUGGLING
FOR SPACE, DEPTH AND BERTH
ALWAYS IN THE DARK AND DAMP
HIDDEN AWAY, DEEP, DEEP,
IN THE ROTTING EARTH.

HEAVEN
GAZE NOT UPWARDS
IN SEEKING HEAVEN
BUT RATHER INWARDLY
FOR YOUR SOUL IS THE GATEWAY
AND NEITHER ORION NOR ADROMEDA
HOLD THE KEY.

SMOOTH
A SMILE AND SENSE OF HUMOUR ARE THE LUBRICANTS TO LIFE.

SEEDS
JUST AS A BITTER SEED
CAN PRODUCE THE SWEETEST FRUIT
AND MOST BEAUTIFUL FLOWER,
SO BITTER STRUGGLE
CAN BE THE CATALYST
TO YOUR FINEST HOUR.

SMILE
THE RIPPLES
EMANATING FROM A SMILE
TRAVEL FAR AND WIDE,
WHILST ANGER'S POISON
DROPS LIKE A STONE
WASHED AWAY BY THE TIDES.

SECRET
GOD WILL NEVER REVEAL
THE SECRETS OF LIFE TO YOU
NO MATTER HOW OFTEN
YOU MAKE THE ATTEMPT
FOR HE KNOWS WELL
THAT FAMILIARITY
BREEDS CONTEMPT.

WAVES
DON'T MAKE WAVES IT IS TOLD,
BY THOSE WHO HAVE NO CONCEPT
AS TO THE DANGERS
THAT STAGNANT WATERS HOLDS.

CRUEL
WHAT WAS HE THINKING
GIVING US BOUNDLESS EMOTIONS
BUT ONLY LIMITED INTELLIGENCE
WITH NO PERSPECTIVE.

TEARS
TEARS OF JOY
FRAGILE AND FICKLE AS LIFE,
ARE ONLY A FILM AWAY
FROM TEARS OF STRIFE.

BEAUTIFUL
EACH LIFE
A UNIQUE TAPESTRY
SMOOTH ON VEVET
PRETTY AS SILK
EMBROIDED WITH THREADS
SILVER AND GOLD
SPRINKLED WITH GLITTER
SO BEAUTIFUL TO BEHOLD.

LUCKY
LUCKY IS THE SOUL
WRAPPED IN AN
INDOMITABLE SPIRIT
COVERED BY AN OPEN MIND
AND HOUSED IN AN INQUISITIVE BRAIN.

ENIGMA

THE ENIGMA WHICH IS MY LIFE
IS BOURNE OUT BY THE FACT
THAT I AM A PART OF THE FLOCK
BUT HAVE NEVER BEEN
ONE OF THE SHEEP,
NOR THE SHEPARD
NOR ANY PART OF HIS KEEP.

DEMOCRACY
IN THE DARK HOURS
OF THE NIGHT
THE VASE HAS FALLEN
FROM A GREAT HEIGHT
SMASHED TO SMITHEREENS
THERE'S NOTHING POSITIVE
HERE TO BE FOUND
BUT IN THE NAME OF SANITY
AND INTELLECT
SEARCH WE ARE BOUND
TO FIND THE SLIGHTEST GLIMMER
OF REASON AND HOPE
AMOUNGST THE SHARDS
NOW LYING ON THE GROUND.

CRUTCH
WHAT DIFFERENCE THE CRUTCH
BE IT THE PROPHECIES OF THE PROPHETS
OR THE POSITIONS OF MARS AND JUPITER
MAYBE THE POTION
OR THROW OF THE DICE
WHAT MATTERS THE CRUTCH
AS LONG AS WE ARE NOT RESPONSIBLE
AND DON'T HAVE TO THINK TWICE.

SPRING MORN

THE SUN IS RISING
SENDING ITS RAYS CASCADING
THROUGH THE WINDOW.
CURTAINS SWAYING GENTLY
IN THE MORNING LAZE.
LIGHT SHADOWING
FLOATING PARTICLES OF DUST
SETTLING ON THE TABLE
WHERE MAGAZINE AND GLASSES
ARE HAPHAZARDLY THRUST
AND LOOK, EACH GLASS A PRISM
BRILLIANT COLOURS
NOW BEING SPRAYED
RAINBOWS OF LIGHT
BOUNCING FROM WALL TO WALL
AND THE BEAUTIFUL BUTTERFLY
SETTLING ON THE SILL
ALSO SMILING AND ENJOYING IT ALL

SIBLING
MY BROTHER,
YOU ARE STANDING IN MY SUN
A CHANGE IN STANCE
EVER SO SLIGHT
WILL ALLOW BOTH OF US
TO ENJOY THE LIGHT.

CLOSED
LIKE BIRDS,
EMOTIONS ARE NOT MEANT
TO BE CAGED IN.

PEACE MAKERS
BEWARE OF THE DOVE,
THE BIRD OF PEACE
LOVE AND TRUST,
FOR I HAVE OBSERVED THEM WELL
AND I AM STILL TO SEE ONE
WHO IS WILLING TO SHARE ITS CRUST.

TRUTH
THE TRUTH IS IN THE BEHOLDERS EYES
IT COMES IN VARIOUS
SHADES, COLOURS AND DYES.

SEEDLINGS
WHEN WE GERMINATED SIDE BY SIDE
AS YOUNG SEEDLINGS IN THE GLADE
YOUR SUFFERING NEVER OCCURRED TO ME
OWING TO MY SHADE
TODAY, THIS THOUGHT MAKES ME COWER
FOR ONLY NOW IN MY LATTER YEARS
AM I ABLE TO APPRECIATE YOUR ROOTS
AND THE MIRACLE WHICH WAS YOUR FLOWER.

SALTY
THE SALTIEST SUBSTANCE
KNOWN TO NATURE
ARE THE TEARS OF THE ORPHAN.

BLIND

THE DARKNESS HAS DESCENDED ON ME
NO LONGER WILL THOSE BEAUTIFUL
SPECKLES OF LIGHT
FIND THE WARM RECEPTION
OF MY SIGHT
BUT MY THOUGHTS REMAIN COLOURED
AND MY HEART IS STILL WARM
FOR INSPITE OF IT ALL, I REMAIN GRATEFUL
FOR THERE ARE WORSE DARKNESSES TO BARE,
SUCH AS THOSE OF INGORANCE
DEPRESSION AND DESPAIR.

SEPERATION
YOU KNOW MY LOVE,
AT SOME STAGE
YOU WILL HAVE TO WALK ALONE
AND YOU WILL DRAW STRENGTH
FROM THE MEMORIES
WHICH WE ARE MAKING TODAY.
SO LETS LIVE OUR LIVES, SO THAT NOTHING
CAN BE MEASURED IN HALVES
AND THE SUSTENANCE THUS DERIVED
WILL BE AS RICH TO YOU
AS CHOLESTRUM IS TO CALVES.

VALUE
WISE IS THE MAN
WHO VALUES THINGS
BEFORE THEY BECOME VALUABLE
AND HOLDS ON TO THEM
EVEN AS THEY BECOME
INVALUABLE.

AFRICAN SPIRIT

CRY AFRICA CRY
FOR YOU DON'T DESERVE YOUR HISTORY
YOUR SHEPERDS HAVE LED YOU TO
RIVER BEDS DRY
BUT THE SUN IS RISING AND THE
SOULS OF YOUR DRUMS
ARE BOTH ANCIENT AND STRONG
SO ARISE SPIRIT AFRICA
FOR IT'S YOUR DESTINY
PAINTED ON ROCK
PULSATING IN YOUR RHYTHMS
VIBRATING IN YOUR SONG.

LIFE
AS FASCINATING AS THE GALAXIES
AND UNIVERSES SEEM TO BE
IT'S THE CREATION OF LIFE
WHICH REMAINS
GODS GREATEST TESTOMANY.

DISTRAUGHT

A CHILD IS DEAD
LEAVING ONE NUMB AND SENSELESS.
IN AN EFFORT TO COMFORT
I CALL ON THE LIKES OF
WORDSWORTH AND SHAKESPEARE,
BUT A QUARTER OF A MILLION WORDS
AT MY DISPOSAL, NOW FILLING MY HEAD,
ARE ALL RENDERED IMPOTENT AND
USELESS
FOR AFTER ALL, DAMN IT, A CHILD IS DEAD.

SHOCK
THE RUDE AWAKENING
AWAITING ALL OF US, AFTER DEATH,
IS FINDING OUT THAT LIFE ON EARTH
WAS THE VACATION,
THE WELL DESEVED REST.

PAUSE
ONCE EVERY NOW AND SO OFTEN
PRESS THE PAUSE BUTTON
AND FREEZE THE FRAME.
STUDY IT WELL
FIX IT IN YOUR MIND WITH CERTAINTY,
FOR NO PRINTS OR PHOTOCOPIES
WILL PASS OVER WITH YOU INTO ETERNITY.

RELEASED
GOD'S RELATIONSHIP TO LIFE
IS ANALAGOUS TO THE BOW
AND ARROW.

FIRST LOVE
THE FIRE FROM A FIRST LOVE
IS SO STRONG
THAT IT CAN BE FELT
OVER THE AGES
EVEN AS LIGHT STRUGGLES
ACROSS CATARACTS WELL FORMED
THE GLOW CAN STILL BE SEEN
AND THE HEART, NOW WEAK,
CAN STILL BE WARMED.

LABYRINTH
LIFE IS LIVED IN A LABYRINTH
EVERY TURN A NEW REALITY
ACCOMPANIED BY ECHOES
FROM THE PAST
AND THE FOOTPRINTS OF THOSE
WHO WENT BEFORE YOU,
IN STONE THEY ARE CAST.

PERSPECTIVE
THE IGNORANCE OF THE FISH
IT MUST BE SAID
DETRACTS NOTHING FROM THE FACT
THAT THE RIVER IS FLOWING
AND THAT THE GREAT OCEAN
STILL LIES AHEAD.

BENIGN

OFTEN DARKNESS IS A THIN VENEER
WHICH CAN BE WIPED AWAY
WITH A SIMPLE SMILE
A THUMBS UP SIGN
OR EVEN A WORD OR TWO
LIKE "I'M SORRY"
OR "IT'S BENIGN"

STABILITY
GOOD MEMORIES OF YOUR YOUTH
ARE YOUR CHOLESTRUM AND YOUR NECTAR
HOPEFULLY BOTH RICH AND SWEET
FOR THEY WILL BE YOUR SUSTENANCE
AS INEVITABLY
THE TRIALS AND TRIBULATIONS OF LIFE
YOU WILL MEET.

STRONG CURRENTS
ONE CANNOT OPPOSE THE STREAM OF LIFE
NOR RESIST THE CURRENT OF TIME
FOR IT'S IN THEIR WATERS
THAT YOU RESIDE
SO, GO WITH THE FLOW AND ENJOY
THE RIDE.

STRENGTH
STRENGTH DERIVED FROM KINDNESS
IS STRONGER THAN STEEL
FORGED IN FIRES FURNACE.

TIME FLIES
THE YEARS ARE MY TREADMILL
FLASHING BENEATH MY FEET
I USED TO COUNT THEM ONCE
STEP BY STEP
EVEN IN MY SLEEP
BUT NOW THE BLURR IS SUCH
THAT IN THE MAIN
IV'E GIVEN UP CARING VERY MUCH
FOR NOW
THE TREADMILL IS MOVING SO FAST
THAT SURELY SOON
MY TIME TOO WILL HAVE PASSED.

LIFE LESSONS

JUST ONE OF THOSE LESSONS
WHICH LIFE TRIES TO TEACH
BUT CLEARLY YOU ARE NOT THERE YET
FOR IN YOUR HAND IS THE VERY BEST
PEACH
AND STILL YOU GAZING LONGINGLY
UPWARDS
AT THE TREE
SEARCHING FOR ALL THE OTHERS
WHICH ARE OUT OF REACH.

GUTS

WE ALL KNOW
THAT IT'S ONLY FOOLS OR THE BRAVE
WHO STAND UP AGAINST THE WIND
AND IT'S THE BLACK SHEEP
WHO FACES THE MUSIC
WHILST THE COWARDS
SHIVER AND CRINGE IN THEIR SLEEP.

NUTRITION
A LIFE FULFILLED
PROVIDES FOR A DEATH
WELL NOURISHED.

SPORES
WITHIN DEATHS ASHES
LIE THE SMOLDERING SPORES
OF LIFE.

AGEING

DESPITE LIFES BEST EFFORTS
MY HAND IS STILL STEADY
AND THERE'S NO TREMOR TO MY VOICE
BUT WHEN I LOOK FORWARDS
THE BRIGHT LIGHT I USED TO SEE
WITH MY HEART AFLAME
IS NOW DIMMING, INTERMITTENLY,
AS IF THE FILM IS SLOWING DOWN
AND I AM BEGINNING TO SEE IT ALL NOW
FRAME BY FRAME.

LOSS

GRATEFUL I WILL ALWAYS BE
FOR A PART OF YOU REMAINS
INBEDDED IN MY MEMORY
EVEN TO THIS DAY
LIKE A BURNING EMBER
KEEPING ME WARM
AND LIGHTING MY WAY.

LOVE

THE WAVE WAS TOO HIGH
THE DELUGE TOO POWERFUL
THERE I WAS ROLLING
OVER AND OVER AND OVER AGAIN
COMMON SENSE DICTATES
THAT THE MOMENTUM WILL SLOW
AND THAT IN TIME
THE ENERGY ITSELF WILL EXPEND
SO UNTIL THEN
HEAD OVER HEELS ROLLING
IN LOVE
OVER AND OVER AGAIN
TO THE VERY LAST MOMENT
I INTEND!

THE HEALER
WHO WILL HEAL THE HEALER?
IS THERE A BALM
TO EASE THE WEIGHT
ON HIS STRAINING SHOULDERS
AND IS THERE A LOTION OR MAYBE A SONG
TO SOOTHE HIS SOUL SO TIRED
OR COULD THERE BE A POTION OR A TONIC
TO LIFT HIS SPIRITS, SO DRAINED AND TRIED
WHICH OF YOU WILL HEAL THIS HEALER
WHO FOR SO LONG NOW HAS SELF DENIED.

HATE
POISONED ARROWS
TIPPED WITH HATE
NEARLY ALWAYS INFECT THOSE
FROM WHENCE THEY ORIGINATE.

INNER SHIELD
LUCKY IS THE MAN
WHO HAS INNER STRENGTH
INNER HAPPINESS, AND INNER PEACE
FOR THAT'S HIS IMMUNITY
TO BOTH LIFE AND DEATHS
PRICKLY REACH.

NO FEAR
I FEAR NO MAN, NOR GOD
NEITHER LIFE NOR DEATH
I FEAR NO OBSTACLE, NOR TEST
ONLY MYSELF, MY INNER SELF,
WHICH REFUSES TO REST.

THE TREE
I HAVE ALWAYS ADMIRED THE PATIENCE
AND TOLERENCE OF THE TREE
I WONDER THOUGH
IF GIVEN THE CHOICE
WOULD IT *STILL* BE?

SEEDS
A HUNGRY MAN YOU MAY FEED
BUT FORGET NOT
THE PARTING GIFT OF SEED.

NIGHTMARES
YES IT'S TRUE THAT
SOMETIMES NIGHTMARES
HAVE THEIR LIGHT OF DAY
BUT LO AND BEHOLD
THEY HAVE THEIR SEASONS TOO
AND ULTIMATELY
FADE AWAY.

FATHER
YOU SAY I'M KIND
BUT MY HEART IS LIKE LEAD
YOU SAY I'M YOUR ROCK
THEN WHY ALL THIS DREAD?
TRUTH BE TOLD MY CHILD
I'M JUST LIKE YOU,
STUMBLING IN THE DARK
ONLY ONE STEP AHEAD.

BIG FISH
THERE WILL ALWAYS BE
A BIGGER FISH THAN YOU
AND PRESENTLY IF THAT'S NOT THE CASE
THEN DON'T WORRY,
TIME KNOWS WHAT TO DO.

TWINKLE

TWINKLE, TWINKLE LITTLE STAR
EVERY NIGHT YOU ARE BADE,
BUT WHEN I SEE THE TWINKLE
IN HER EYES,
IT LEAVES YOU STANDING
IN THE SHADE!

LOVE
NO EXTERNAL FORCE
CAN DESTROY LOVE
ONLY THE HEART
WHICH GAVE IT BIRTH
CAN BE THE CONDITIONER
THEREOF.

BREATH
TAKE A BREATH
TAKE A BREATHER
WHAT THE HELL,
FILL YOUR LUNGS
YOU ONLY LIVE ONCE!

SILENCE

I KNOW YOU CAN'T HEAR ME
BUT STILL I TALK TO YOU
THE SILENT ECHO
WILL JUST HAVE TO DO.
I OFTEN THINK OF YOU
IN THAT PLACE,
SO DISTANT AND SO SILENT
AND I MUST TELL YOU
THAT I WOULD FORFEIT EVERYTHING
THAT IS MINE
IN ORDER TO SEE YOUR SMILE
FOR JUST ONE MORE TIME.

WITNESS
IF ONLY THEY COULD TALK
EACH ROCK A WITNESS
EVERY PEBBLE POLISHED BY HISTORY
AND EVERY STONE
WITH IT'S INCREDIBLE STORY.

CAREFUL
ABOVE ALL THINGS
REMEMBER THAT THE LIGHT
KNOWS NO EMOTION.

THOUGHTS
IN ALL CREATION
THE GIFTS OF THOUGHT
AND MEMORY
WERE GIVEN ONLY TO YOU
AND NO OTHER,
USE THEM WELL
THINK GOOD THOUGHTS
THINK IN COLOUR.

ASPHYXATON
HATE AND JEALOUSY
CONSUME ALL THE OXYGEN
IN THEIR PROXIMITY
STRANGLING ANY HOPE OF
CLARITY OF THOUGHT
AND MEASURED SENSIBILITY.

THE BOOK
OH BLESSED BOOK
TAKE ME AWAY
FOR JUST A FEW MOMENTS
LET ME FLY, LET ME SMILE
AND LET ME CRY.
OH BLESSED BOOK
TAKE ME IN
FOR JUST A FEW MOMENTS
LET ME BELIEVE, LET ME HOPE
AND LET ME DREAM

MOOD
I MUST TELL YOU
THAT THIS MOOD IS NOTHING MORE
THAN A HIGH TIDE ON A CLOUDY DAY,
AND WE ALL KNOW THAT THE TIDE EBBS
AND THAT CLOUDS ARE NOMADS
AND NEVER STAY.

GRAN
WHEN I LOOK IN YOUR EYES
I SEE SUCH WISDOM
BOTH ANCIENT AND TIRED
SOMETIMES WHEN YOU GLANCE
IN MY DIRECTION AND SMILE
IT'S LIKE GOD HIMSELF
IS CRADELING ME LIKE A CHILD.

TRUTH
SOMETIMES
OUR HEARTS AND OUR MINDS
SEE THE TRUTH IN DIFFERING LIGHTS
WHICH TO SWEAR MY ALLEGENCE TO
ON WHICH TO SET MY SIGHTS?

JUDGES
JUDGE ME FROM YOUR SAFE HEIGHTS
IF YOU WILL
BUT REJOICE NOT QUITE YET
FOR THE WATERS ARE RISING FAST
AND SOON
YOUR FEET TOO WILL BE WET.

TWILIGHT
TWILIGHT
NARCOIC SUNDOWNER
MASKING THE TRUTH
THAT AFTER THIS CALM
COMES THE NIGHT
AND THEN THE MORROW
WITH ALL ITS DEPARTURES
AND INEVITABLE SORROWS.

LOVE BITES
I WOULD HAVE THOUGHT
THAT LOVE WOULD BE OPEN
TO ALL OTHER LOVES,
WELCOMING THEM WITH OPEN ARMS,
BUT ALAS NO!
AS IT TURNS OUT IN THIS LIGHT
LOVE IS TOTALLY INTOLERENT,
JEALOUSLY GUARDING ITS POSSESSIONS
AND ALL IN ITS SIGHT,
CONSTANTLY MARKING ITS BORDERS
BRIGHTLY COLOURED IN RED.
IT APPEARS, THAT IN ORDER
FOR THIS LOVE TO SURVIVE,
I HAVE TO OBLITERATE
ABSOLUTELY AND COMPLETELY,
ALL MY OTHER LOVES,
ESPECIALLY, THOSE WHICH
STILL ARE IN MY HEAD.

LETHARGY

MY SOUL HAS A TENDENCY
TO LETHARGY
I WISH IT WOULD CLIMB
TO HIGHER HEIGHTS
OR FLY OFF TO EXOTIC SIGHTS
BUT NO,
IT APPEARS TO HAVE FOUND ITS PLACE,
BOTH WARM AND COMFORTABLE
IN MY TIRING BODY,
HAPPLIY,
LEAVING ALL THE WORRYING
AND FRETTING UP TO ME!

NEW DAY

COME NOW, OPEN YOUR EYES
OPEN THE SHUTTERS AND THE BLINDS
FOR A NEW DAWN IS ON ITS WAY.
SCARRED AND FATIGUED
FROM ITS LONG BATTLE WITH THE NIGHT,
IT'S RESTING ON THE HORISON NOW
LICKING ITS WOUNDS
BASKING IN AMBIENT LIGHT.
BUT SOON IT WILL ARISE
TRIUMPHANT AND HAPPY
SO COME NOW, OPEN YOUR EYES
FOR JOYOUSLY
A NEW DAY HAS ARRIVED.

RELUCTANCE
YES THE WATER'S COLD
AND THE POOL IS DEEP,
BUT YOU KNOW THERE'S
ONLY ONE WAY ACROSS
SO COME ON MATE,
IN YOU LEAP!

LINDSAY
FOR ONE MOMENT
THE FIRST TIME I SAW YOUR FACE
TIME CAUGHT ITS BREATH
SMILED AND STOOD COMPLETELY STILL.

LOVERS
IS IT INDELIBLY SO
THAT THE LIGHT AND DARK
WILL ALWAYS BE FOES?
COULD THEY NOT BE FRIENDS,
OR EVEN BETTER STILL LOVERS,
DANCING AROUND EACH OTHER
TO A SONG THAT NEVER ENDS.

PARTICLES
SO WE ARE PARTICLES ON THE WIND;
WHAT THEN IS THE SCORE,
WHEN THE WIND DROPS,
OR EVEN WORSE
BLOWS UP A STORM?

WAKE UP CALL
TAKE HEED AND LEARN
FROM THE ANTS AND THE BEES
FOR LOUNGING AROUND
AND WATCHING TV
IS DEFINITELY NOT
WHAT GOD NEEDS.

SOULS
NO TWO SOULS ARE THE SAME
LIKE FINGERPRINTS
ON THE WIND.

GRAVE
WHY IS YOUR GRAVE SO SILENT
NEITHER VIBRATION NOR WHISPER,
HOW CAN THIS BE?
SURELY SOMETHING TO BE SAID?
OR CAN IT BE,
THAT MAYBE, JUST MAYBE,
YOU REALLY ARE DEAD?

THE TREE

THE STORM CAME
RIPPING ALL ASUNDER
SPREADING DEVASTATION
IN A VISCOUS PLUNDER.
BUT IN ITS RAGE AND BLIND FURY,
IT COULD NOT GET HOLD OF ME,
WELL HIDDEN AND PROTECTED
BY THE BOUGHS
OF THE GREAT ELM TREE.
BUT NOW MANY YEARS HAVE PASSED
ANOTHER HOLOCAUST IS ON ITS WAY
WOODCUTTERS IN THE AREA
WITH EVER TREE UNDER THEIR GAZE
SO HERE, ONCE AGAIN I SIT IN THE BOUGHS
OF THIS GREAT ELM TREE
FOR ANYONE WANTING TO HARM MY
FRIEND
WILL FIRST HAVE TO DEAL WITH ME!

LAST CHANCE
SAY WHAT YOU WANT TO ME NOW,
FOR WHERE I AM GOING
THE DEAF REIGN
THE TONGUE IS MUTE
AND I BELIEVE THE BLIND THERE
FEEL WELL AT HOME TOO.

NOVA

THE TWILIGHT HAS ARRIVED
AND SOON MY TIME WILL BE OVER
I WANT YOU TO KNOW
THAT NO LIGHT
HAS EVER SHONE BRIGHTER
YOU ARE ALWAYS MY SUPERNOVA.

THE SMILE

I HAVE SPENT MOST OF MY LIFE
SMILING IT AWAY
THERE ARE THOSE WHO SAY
I COULD HAVE DONE BETTER
RUN FASTER, CLIMBED HIGHER
NOW THAT I AM APPROACHING OLD AGE
WHERE EVERYTHING NARROWS
AND SPEEDS UP AT THE SAME TIME
I BEG TO DIFFER
I'M STILL SMILING!

DEFINITION
JUST AS THE DARK CONTRASTS
THE LIGHT
AND COLOURS HIGHLIGHT THE WHITE
SO DEATH TOO DEFINES A LIFE.

FINDING GOD
THROUGH THE MICROSCOPE
I CAN SEE BILLIONS OF PARTICLES
IN A STATE OF ENTROPY
BUT IN REVERSE,
NOT ONE OF THEM CAN SEE ME.

THE DEAL
THE HAND WAS DEALT
THE UNDERSTANDING CLEAR
IN RETURN FOR NINETY YEARS
I WOULD GO QUIETLY, WITHOUT A FUSS
A SMILE ON MY FACE AND A PLEASANT CHEER.

PASSING
MY FOLKS HAVE PASSED
NOW PREFIXED AS "LATE"
SOMEHOW, I FIND IT EASIER NOW
TO COME TO TERMS
WITH MY OWN INEVTABLE FATE.

FEAR
FEAR OF THE FUTURE
DISTRACTS FROM THE PRESENT
FEAR OF THE UNKNOWN
DISTURBS ONES SPIRIT
FEAR OF DEATH
DETRACTS FROM LIFE
FEAR DISTORTS AND BLURRS REALITY
WASTES PRECIOUS TIME
A TOXIC INSANITY.

PASSING THE TORCH
SO FRUSTRATING TO SIT NEXT
TO THIS OLD MAN HOLDING THE REIGNS
WITH HIS EYES GLASSY AND TIRED
SO SCARED TO PASS OVER CONTROL
TO THIS YOUNG MAN NEXT TO ME
WITH HIS EYES RESTLESS AND ON FIRE.

<u>WASTE</u>
PLAYER OF TIME
SILLY FOOL
WASTING AWAY
YOUTH'S PRECIOUS POOL.

STORMY
LIFE AND THE UNIVERSE
ARE BOTH WHIRLWINDS
ULTIMATELY THE DUST SETTLES.

THE "L" PRINCIPLE

EL
∧
LEVITATE
∧
LABYRINGTH
∧
LIGHT, LOVE
∧
LEARNING, LISTENING
∧
LABOUR, LAUGHTER, LEISURE

ENVY
HOW I ENVY YOUR YOUTH
AND COVET YOUR TIME.

IN SYNC

PHEROMONE CRAZED
ARMY OF ANTS
KILLING AND DESTROYING
EVERY TERMITE IN SIGHT
EVEN THE INNOCENT PUPAE
DISPATCHED WITH ONE SINGLE BITE.
FRENZIED, INSANE HORNETS
ATTACKING AND KILLING
WHOLE HIVES OF BEES
WITHOUT ANY PROVOCATION
WANTON SLAUGHTER
ON A MASSIVE SCALE
WITH DEVASTATING EASE
AND US
"LOVE THY NEIGHBOUR" WE ARE TAUGHT
"TURN THE OTHER CHEEK"
ARE WE OUT OF SYNC
SECOND GUESSING NATURES DECREES?

THE CHOSEN
CONSTANTLY SEARCHING,
VERY RESTLESS,
ALWAYS INSECURE,
SKEPTICAL, ARROGANT
NEVER SATISFIED
– GODS CHOSEN.

ARISTOCRACY
THEIR EYES WERE WIDE OPEN
THEIR MOUTHS WERE ALWAYS OPEN
EVEN THEIR MINDS WERE OPEN
BUT ALAS,
THEIR HEARTS AND HANDS
WERE CLOSED

POISON

I HAVE TRIED JEALOUSY, SELFISHNESS,
I HAVE UNLEASHED MY EGO
DISCOVERED THE WORD ME
I CAN TELL YOU IT STINGS, IT BURNS,
FOR THESE ARE ALL TOXIC CAGES
AND MY SOUL NEEDS TO BE FREE

JOURNEY'S END
AS THE WAX BURNS
NEARLY TO THE GROUND
I FIND MY SOUL HOLDING TIGHT
ONTO CHERISHED MEMORIES
WHICH I INTEND TAKING WITH ME
ON CROSSING THE SHROUD

ORIGINS
MAN LOOKS UP
AT ORION WITH NOSTALGIA
AND FASCINATION
FOR INSTINCTIVELY HE KNOWS
THEREIN LIES HIS ORIGINS
AND FINAL DESTINATION.

FINGERPRINTS
FINGERPRINTS
OUR BIOLOGICAL DOCUMENT
CONTAINING ALL OUR HISTORIES,
ALBEIT IN CODE
EASILLY SCANNED
BY THOSE IN THE KNOW.

LINAMENT
JUST AS COOL WATER
SOOTHES A PARCHED THROAT
SO MEMORIES OF MY YOUTH
HEAL MY SOUL.

SENSELESS

A MYRIAD OF FLAVOURS
BOUQUETS AND COLOURS
TO CHOOSE FROM
AND YET LIFE DEPENDANT WATER
IS ODORLESS, COLOURLESS AND TASTLESS
HAS TO BE A GOOD REASON
NATURE'S USUALLY SPOT ON!

FAITH
LOOKING UP YOU SEE A BRIGHT STAR
THEN CLOUDS MOVE IN AND COVER IT
BUT THE STAR'S STILL THERE.
THEN DAWN BREAKS
SUNLIGHT ERASING ALL TO BE SEEN
BUT THE STAR'S STILL THERE.
THEN YOU LOOSE INTEREST AND
STOP LOOKING AT IT
BUT THE STAR'S STILL THERE.

THE ROSE
OF LIGHT AND DARK FORCES
THEOLOGINS SPEAK
LIGHT AND DARK ENERGY
SCIENTISTS SEEK
"A ROSE BY ANY OTHER NAME
WOULD SMELL AS SWEET"

THE MOON
WHICH IS IT TO BE
A DEAD USELESS ROCK
CAPTURED BY THE EARTHS GRAVITY
OR A BEAUTIFUL BACKDROP
TO ROMANCE
SOOTHING WAVES
DREAMS AND FANTASIES?

RAMSGATE
I AM LONG GONE
AND THE WAVES STILL ROLL
ONTO RAMSGATE BEACH
THE SEAGULLS STILL SQUABBLE
OVER SCRAPS OF FISH
AND THE WAFFLES FROM THE HUT
ESPECIALLY THE CHOC AND COCONUT
STILL DELIGHTING ALL YOU MEET.

MY LOVE
IF THE SOLE PURPOSE TO MY EXISTENCE
IS TO GUIDE YOU ON YOUR JOURNEY
AS BOTH SEED AND SOWER,
THEN MY LOVE,
MY CUP RUNNETH OVER.

ALONE
LAYER UPON LAYER
BOTH SHROUD AND CRUTCH
BUT IN THE END
WHEN ALL FALLS AWAY
AND FADES OUT OF SIGHT
IT'S YOU AND YOU ALONE
FACING THE INEVITABLE NIGHT.

PARTING

IT'S STILL RAINING OUT
TORRENTS, SHEETS OF WATER
FALLING FROM THE SKY,
YET MY THROAT IS TIGHT
AND MY MOUTH IS DRY,
THE TEAR ON YOUR CHEEK SAYS IT ALL
AND I TELL YOU MY LOVE,
IT'S DRENCHING MY HEART,
DROWNING MY SOUL,
TIME NOW TO SAY GOODBYE
TO RELEASE CONTROL.

BITTER
THE PILL OF ANGER
SWALLOWED IN SUCH HASTE
HAS NO ANTIDOTE TO
ITS BITTER TASTE.

PERSPECTIVE
LITTLE ANT
HOW TO EXPLAIN TO YOU
THE MAGNIFICENCE OF BURGUNDY?
LITTLE MAN
HOW TO EXPLAIN TO YOU
THE MAGNIFICENCE OF ETERNITY?

THE CHALLENGE
HOW TO MAINTAIN
THE INNOCENCE
THE OPTIMISM
THE WONDERMENT
THE ANTICIPATION
THE SHEER JOY OF A CHILD
THE AGING MIND HARDENS IT SEEMS
AND REALIZES THAT
THE DREAM WAS ONLY A DREAM.

PROGRAMMED
LET'S CUT TO THE CHASE
CALL A SPADE A SPADE
YOU ARE BORN
PROGRAMMED TO DIE
WHAT A GREAT KICK- START TO LIFE
TALK ABOUT A CURVED BALL!
TRIED LOOKING AT THIS
AS A HALF CUP FULL
RIGHT FOOT FORWARDS
POSITIVE SPIN
HEALTHY ATTITUDE
HOLISM, YOGA, MEDITATION
EVEN A TOUCH OF RELIGION
BUT NOTHING SOFTENS THE FACT
THAT YOU ARE BORN
PROGRAMMED TO DIE
AND THAT MY FRIEND, IS THAT!

EYE ROLL
SELF CONFIDENCE
BUILT UP OVER MANY YEARS
AT SOME TOLL
DESTROYED IN A BLINK
BY ONE PRETTY EYE ROLL

SHORT
NOT EVEN A BLINK
NOT A BLURR, NOR A SMUDGE
JUST A FLEETING SHADOW
A FIGMENT
A TOUCH
FLICKERED, THEN GONE
MY LIFE.

HOMELESS
LIFE STANDS OPPOSED
PRICKING AND SCRATCHING
LIKE A THORNY HEDGE
COLD PAVEMENTS MY HOME
EMPTY BOTTLES MY CURRENCY
I'M ON THE EDGE.

ADULTHOOD
BEAMS AND PILLARS NO MORE
STRUTS REMOVED
GUIDE ROPES LOOSENED
SCAFFOLDING LOWERED TO THE FLOOR
NOW LET'S SEE IF THE STRUCTURE
CAN WITHSTAND
THE OPENING OF THIS DOOR?

DREAMS

WHY SHOULDN'T I HAVE
MY HEAD IN THE CLOUDS
AND MY ASPIRATIONS
IN THE STARS
GOD KNOWS
IT BEATS ANYTHING ON THE GROUND

IN HIS IMAGE
NEITHER SPIRIT
NOR LIGHT
BUT FALLIBLE BIOLOGY
"AND ON THE SEVENTH DAY HE RESTED"

THE ROCK
LUCKY IS THE CHILD
WHO LOOKS UP AND SEES
GIBRALTA
FOR THERE ARE TOO MANY
WHO ONLY SEE
THE SHADOW OF THE WAVE
CURLING OVER SAND- CASTLES
AS THEY FALTER.

DOWN
MELANCHOLY IS OFTEN
A MALNUTRITION OF THE SOUL
AS SUCH, IT CAN BE
HEALED BY SOFT MUSIC,
GOOD COMPANY AND
A GREAT CASEROLE.

DEMOCRACY LOST
AS HUMANS WE ASPIRE TO
Liberté, égalité, fraternité
TAUGHT THAT ALL ARE BORN EQUAL
BUT THIS IS NOT NATURE'S WAY
AND AFTER DEATH?
A SMALL MINORITY OF SOULS
CLIMB THE MOUNTAIN
EVEN FEWER SIT AT HIS FEET
THE VAST MAJORITY
DEVIDED BETWEEN SEVEN LEVELS
OF ABSOLUTE INEQUALITY
NO DEMOCRACY HERE TO BE SEEN.

WASTE OF TIME
DEPRESSION
THAT SEDUCTIVE WRAP
I HAVE TRIED IT IN SMALL DOSES
DURING MY WAKING DAY
AND IN COPIOUS AMOUNTS
DURING NIGHTS OF DISARRAY
DEPRESSION
I HAVE COME TO CONCLUDE
IS A BLOODY WASTE OF TIME
A MIRAGE, IN MALICIOUS SUBTERFUGE.

DETOUR
NOT EVERY ADVANCE IS PROGRESS
AND NOT EVERY REVERSE A DEFEAT
SOMETIMES
THE QUICKEST ROUTE TO SUCCESS
IS FOUND BY INITIATING
A RETREAT

ALL THINGS PASS
ALL TOO SOON
THE NEW FLAVOUR
BECOMES BLAND
THE FLAMES OF PASSION
BURN DOWN TO THE GROUND
BLINK AND THE BEAUTIFULL SEASHELL
IS COVERED BY THE SAND
THIS IS NATURES WAY
THERE'S NO OTHER WAY AROUND

SORRY
I SAW THE WORDS LEAVING MY LIPS
ENROUTE TO YOU
I GRABBED AT THEM
BUT TO NO AVAIL,
FOR THEY HIT THEIR TARGET
WELL AND TRUE!

LIFE
LIFE IS ONE ORGANISM
WITH A COLLECTIVE MEMORY- INSTINCT
AND A UNIFIED GOAL
SURVIVAL.

POLITICIANS
JUST AS DARK CLOUDS
SHADOW SILVER LINNINGS
IN THE SKIES
SO, BEHIND EVERY PROMISE
BEWARE OF THE LIES.

GUILT
GUILT CAN BE SO HEAVY
THAT IT CAN CREATE
BLACK HOLES.

CYCLES
**DUST TO DUST
WOMB TO WOMB
LIGHT TO LIGHT.**

FORWARDS
LIFE'S STRONG CURRENT
IS RELENTLESS
SWEEPING FORWARDS
NO PAUSE, NO REPLAY
NO REVISITING THE PAST
NOT EVEN ONE NOSTALGIC
BACKWARDS GLANCE
FORWARDS.

THE GIFT
THE BEST GIFT
I HAVE GIVEN YOU
IS THAT THERE IS NOTHING
YOU NEED FROM ME
NOW.

CANDLE
LIFE
IS ANALOGOUS TO A CANDLE
AS LONG AS THERE'S WAX TO BURN
YOU WILL CONTINUE TO LIVE YOUR TURN.

SOCIALISM
ADMIRE THE LAWN,
BUT FORGET NOT
THE BLADE OF GRASS.

THE KEY
SOLVING THE RIDDLE TO INFINITY,
WILL ALLOW TIME TO BECOME OUR TOOL
AND REACHING THE STARS A REALITY.

ENERGY TRANSFER
IF ENERGY IS CONVERTIBLE TO TIME,
THEN ALL OUR STRUGGLES
ARE CREATING ETERNITY.

THE SPIRIT ENDURES
ONCE AGAIN, I HEARD YOUR WISPER
IN THE JERUSALEM HILLS
SENSED YOUR PRESENCE
AMOUNGST THE PINE TREES
FELT YOUR CARESS
ON THE WIND
SO STILL.

TRUTH BE TOLD
AT SOME STAGE
THE SMILE
BECOMES MORE IMPORTANT
THAN THE PRETTY FACE.

FIREWALL
THERE ARE REASONS
FOR THE FIREWALL
BETWEEN LIFE AND DEATH
IN THE MAIN
TO AVOID APATHY
AND TO STIMULATE INTELLECT.

SHADOWS
HOW WHITE IS WHITE?
HOW BRIGHT IS BRIGHT?
HOW LIGHT IS LIGHT?
ONLY THE DARK KNOWS
AS IT'S SHADOW GROWS.

WHITE WAKE

"KEEP A WHITE WAKE"
EASILLY SAID AND DONE
IF YOU LIVE YOUR LIFE ON A PLACID LAKE
OR MEANDERING STREAM
BUT SOME LIVE THEIR LIVES ON HIGH SEAS
AND CHOPPY RAGGING RIVERS
THEIR WAKES ARE MUDDIED AND CHURNED
INSIDE AND OUT - NO WHITE TO BE FOUND
HERE
ALBEIT THOUROUGHLY DESERVED.

CONTINUIM

LIFE AND DEATH ARE AN UNITERRUPTED
CONTINUIM ON THE SAME PATH
OF A MUCH LONGER JOURNEY.
SOME RECOGNIZE THIS EARLY
AND OTHERS MUCH LATER
BUT MOST ARE NEVER THE WISER
PITY, SINCE AWARENESS OF THIS
CAN BE QUITE A TRANQUILIZER.

GRASS IS GREENER
FOOL IS THE MAN
WHO COMPARES LIVES
COVETS FATES
AND COMPETES FOR DESTINIES
FOR SELDOM DO PERCEPTIONS
MIRROR THE REALITIES.

MODERATION
WHILST AIMING HIGH
IS AN ADMIRABLE ACTIVITY
KEEP IN MIND
THAT STRIVING FOR PERFECTION
CAN LEAD TO INSANITY.

PERSPECTIVE
ZOOM OUT AND OUT AND OUT.
LOOK BACK FROM AFAR
LOOKS LIKE A STRAND OF DNA
ZOOM OUT EVEN FURTHER
IS THAT A JAR??

PHILOSOPHY
PHILOSOPHY NEEDS GREATER PERSPECTIVE THAN LIFE CAN PROVIDE

CHALLENGED
LIFE AFTER DEATH
INTELLECTUAL ECLIPSE
LOGIC'S ABYSS

STRUGGLE
HE WHO STRUGGLES
IS VALUED THE MOST
FOR HIS NECTAR
IS THE SWEETEST.

RICH LIFE
REACH OUT AND TOUCH THE DEW,
PUT IT TO YOUR LIPS AND TASTE IT,
SMELL ITS SWEET FRESHNESS
SUFFICE NOT WITH JUST THE VIEW.

UNIQUE

THE CONSENSUS APPEARS TO BE
THAT DEATH IS THE GREAT EQUALIZER
THIS IS NOT TRUE
WHEN ALL IS SAID AND DONE
AS WITH LIFE, EACH DEATH IS UNIQUE
WITH ITS OWN ALGORITHM,
AND INDEPENDENT OUTCOME.

PRAYER
I WOULD PREFER
AN OPEN DIALOGUE UP THERE
RATHER THAN THIS PSYCOPHANTIC
MONOLOGUE DOWN HERE
CALLED PRAYER.

THE KEY
OPEN YOUR EYES,
OPEN YOUR HANDS,
OPEN YOUR HEART,
OPEN YOUR MIND,
HEAVEN'S GATES
NOW WIDE OPEN.

THE FRUIT
THE YOUNG GIRL
IS THE OPENING FLOWER
BEAUTIFUL AND ATTRACTIVE
THE ELDERLY WOMAN
IS THE PROMISED FRUIT.

SABRA
OUR ROOTS RUN DEEP
AND WE WILL NOT BE MOVED.
BLOW US A GALE
AND WE WILL BEND WITH THE WINDS
UNDERSTAND OUR RESOLVE
AND YOU WILL SEE
IT'S THE SAME AS THE ANCIENT CEDAR TREE
AND NOT FICKLE,
LIKE THE JUMPING FLEE.

SCREENS

THE WORDS ARE MY ESCAPE
AND THE SONGS MY SHIELD
THE SMILE A SCREEN
FROM MY INNER SELF
WHICH REFUSES TO HEAL.

LUCKY CHILD.

ARM AROUND THE SHOULDER
WARM LAP TO SNUGGLE
SHOULDER TO REST
HAND IN HAND
BEAR-LIKE HUG
ASSURING WINK
PROUD SMILE
SAFE

LINDSAY
ONE UNIQUE CHANCE TO LIVE
BY ACCIDENT OR BY DESIGN
NEVER AGAIN TO BE REPEATED
ONCE ONLY AND THEN OVER, FOREVER.
BUT NEVER FORGOTTEN
MEMORIES AND LOVE ETCHED INDELIBLY
ON OUR SOULS TO ALL ETERNITY.
WHAT A GIFT
TO HAVE SHARED MY ONLY LIFE WITH YOU
BLESSED FOR SURE!

THE BRAVE

WE COME FROM THE WOMB
OF THE BRAVE
BY THEIR EXAMPLE
WE LIVE OUR LIVES WITH RESOLVE
TRUTH AND COURAGE
WILL FACE OUR DEATHS, STOICALLY,
KNOWING THAT WE ARE RETURNING
TO THE LOVING EMBRACE
OF THE BRAVE.

WOMB
DEATH IS A BIRTH
I BELIEVE THIS TO BE TRUE
LIFE IS LIVED IN A WOMB
SAFE AND WARM TO BE SURE
THIS MEANS THE REAL BEGINNING
LIES BEFORE YOU.

REVELATION

AGE WEARS DOWN THE EGO
OPENING THE WAY TO REALIZATION
THAT YOU ARE JUST ONE OF TRILLIONS
AND TRILLIONS OF ORGANISMS
EQUALLY IMPORTANT
AND EQUALLY IRRELAVENT.
NOT A COMFORTING REVELATION.

HAPPINESS
HAPPINESS CAN ENDURE
BY NOT ALLOWING
THE CYNICISM OF AGE
TO FADE THE COLOURS
AND DULL THE MEMORIES
OF YOUR VIBRANT YOUTH

SAVE AS
ALL THE WONDERFUL THINGS
YOU LOVE TO SEE, SMELL, TOUCH
TASTE, HEAR, IMAGINE
REMEMBER THEM WELL
ENTRENCH THEM IN YOUR MIND
MELD THEM INTO YOUR SOUL
FOR MAKE NO DOUBT
WHERE YOU ARE GOING, THESE THINGS
CAN ONLY BE DREAMED ABOUT.

THE FINAL WORD
AND FINALLY, ON THE STONE
"EVER BATTERED AS AN ISLE
HE SANG THE SONG
WALKED THE WALK
AND SMILED THE SMILE"

www.ingramcontent.com/pod-product-compliance
Lightning Source LLC
Chambersburg PA
CBHW042131160426
43199CB00021B/2878